BANNERS FOR
Visual Worship

70 Designs
Based on the *Lutheran Service Book*

Carla Krazl

CONCORDIA PUBLISHING HOUSE · SAINT LOUIS

To our God, who made our eyes to see,
our minds to appreciate what we see,
and our hearts to feel what we see.

Copyright © 2008 Concordia Publishing House
3558 S. Jefferson Avenue
St. Louis, MO 63118-3968
1-800-325-3040 • www.cph.org

Written by Carla Krazl
Illustrated by Carla Krazl

Manufactured in the United States of America

1 2 3 4 5 6 7 8 9 10   17 16 15 14 13 12 11 10 09 08

Contents

> **Note:** *These banner designs are labeled for use in specific instances. However, many can be used at other times, for other occasions, or for general use. Don't let display of these banners be restricted by the headings given to them.*

Preface

Visual art has been a part of worship since King Solomon built the Lord's temple (1 Kings 6 and 7). From beautiful mosaics of the third century to Michelangelo's painting of the Sistine Chapel in 1512, art has been made to "realize" Christianity and enhance worship.

Artwork is still a powerful aspect of worship today. Church banners convey a quick message in a beautiful vehicle and have impact that words cannot achieve. Banners can tell a story with imagery in a way that broadens scope and widens worship.

The banners in this book are based on the icons and emblems used in the *Lutheran Service Book* that center around a symmetrical cross. The debossed cross in the center of the design reminds us of the darkness of Good Friday. The gold foil cross reminds us of our Lord's resurrection. The eight squares around the cross remind us of Christ's resurrection on Sunday, the eighth day. As a whole, the "design gives the impression of ongoing expansion—even as the Gospel continues to be proclaimed until the end of time ' . . . and to the end of the earth' (Acts 1:8)" (*Lutheran Service Book*, page ix).

Your congregation, too, can experience God's gifts to Christians through their eyes. Set your hands to work for visual worship. To God be the glory!

Construction Guidelines

Selecting a banner to make is sometimes the most difficult part of the project. The table of contents categorizes the banners for quick reference. If your celebration is somewhat nonspecific (praise, family life, etc.), flip through this book and look for possibilities under other sections. Some banners are appropriate for more than one occasion. One consideration as you choose which design to construct should be whether the banner (or group of banners) will appropriately fit in the designated hanging location. If the banner is to be a gift for someone, ask about his or her preferences.

Can't decide? Often the best choice is the banner design that comes to life in your imagination—the one you can already picture in color. Find inspiration by looking at the colorful banner samples on the enclosed CD-ROM. Keep in mind that this is your creation. Feel free to modify a design if it does not look quite "right."

Getting Started

Enlarging the Pattern

After choosing a banner design, the next step is to enlarge the line drawing to a full-size pattern. It is best (and easiest, in the long run) to have **two** full-size patterns. One will be used as a pattern for cutting fabric to the appropriate shapes; the other will be used as a guide for placing the pieces on the banner background.

Enlarging can be done in any of four ways:

1. Printing a Pattern from Your Computer

The easiest option for obtaining a pattern for your banner is to print one directly from the enclosed CD-ROM. Each banner design is on the disk as a simple, black line PDF file just as it appears in the book. Insert the CD in the disk drive, navigate to a category folder, and locate the specific pattern, and double-click it. The pattern will open in Adobe® Reader®. (Adobe Reader must be installed on your computer. System requirements, a download link, and additional information are found in the Read Me file on the CD.) With the banner pattern open, follow your normal procedure to print the file. If your printer uses 8½ × 11-inch paper, choose the **Size to Fit** option in the print dialog box to print a pattern the same size as shown in this book.

Print a full-size pattern by selecting and printing one 8½ × 11-inch section at a time. All the PDF files on the CD are 18 inches wide, so keep this in mind when choosing to print at 100%. (The lengths of the banners vary.)

Now click on **Tools** in the menu bar, pull down to **Select & Zoom**, then choose the **Snapshot Tool**. Drag the crosshairs to highlight the 8½ × 11-inch area you want to print. Choose **Print,** and repeat this procedure for each section of the pattern.

Be certain to organize all the sections as they print, so they may be taped together to make a full-size pattern. It is helpful to have the horizontal and vertical rulers turned on.

2. Using a Projector

Chances are that an opaque projector or overhead projector is available in the church or school office. An opaque projector displays the original design onto paper taped to the wall. An overhead projector does the same but uses a copy of the design photocopied onto a transparency (also available from the church office or a quick-copy store).

Project the banner design onto a blank wall in a semidark room. Move the projector toward or away from the wall to change the size of the image. Use a tape measure to be exact and ensure the projection is "square" (fig. 1). Tape a piece of butcher paper (or disposable tablecloth, wrapping paper, or even sheets of newsprint) to the wall and trace the design. Turn off the projector and look at the finished pattern to make sure nothing has been missed. This pattern will remain uncut and serve as the "placement pattern."

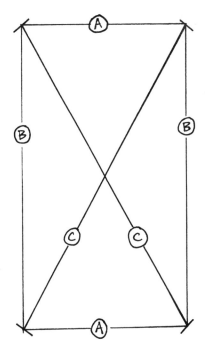

Figure 1. The measurements of opposite sides should be equal. Diagonal measurements should be equal.

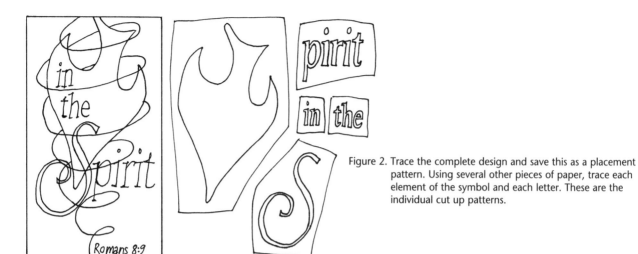

Figure 2. Trace the complete design and save this as a placement pattern. Using several other pieces of paper, trace each element of the symbol and each letter. These are the individual cut up patterns.

Take down your placement pattern and tape up another piece of paper. This time, carefully trace all elements except the plain (nondecorative) letters. Instead, draw a box around them. Check for missing elements and remove the pattern. This "cut-up pattern" will be used to cut the design pieces from fabric. Try to avoid folding the patterns. Roll them up and hold them with a rubber band or roll them around an empty wrapping-paper roll.

Back to those omitted letters . . . trace them onto separate paper. They will be used individually, so paper scraps can be used for these patterns. Be sure all the letters get traced (fig. 2).

3. Using a Photocopier

A photocopier in the church office or at a quick-copy store will have a "zoom" option that will enlarge the pattern as it copies. To find the percentage at which to copy, divide the height of the finished banner by the height of the small banner pattern. Use this number as the percentage for the enlargement. Photocopy the small pattern section by section and tape the pages together to make the full-size pattern.

You may need to enlarge the pattern in two steps. For example, make the first enlargement copy at 250% and tape it together. Then make a second one at 350% of the first enlargement copy for the final, full-size pattern.

4. Using a Grid

No projector? No problem. True, this method is a bit more time consuming, but the advantage is that the design can be easily modified to fit your ideas.

Photocopy both the design from the book and the grid pattern on page 90. Tape the design over the grid so the pages line up and you can see the grid through the design. Determine the size of your finished banner. For example, one grid square could be equal to 6 inches of your finished full-size banner. Keeping equal proportions, lightly draw a larger grid onto butcher (or similar) paper using a yardstick. (A tile floor is often an ideal place to do this because the tiles provide a "square" pattern.) Make sure your pattern is square by measuring diagonals (fig. 1). With the grid lines as your guide, use a pencil to enlarge the design onto the butcher paper. Don't be shy about using an eraser!

A duplicate pattern should be made as outlined in "Using a Projector." An easy way to accomplish this is by laying tissue paper over the enlarged design and tracing carefully.

Choosing Fabric

The fabric store can be an overwhelming place. The best thing to do is to take some time to browse. Make sure to have your design in hand! When choosing a background fabric, notice how different types of fabrics hang. Some heavyweight fabrics, such as cotton duck and denim, heavy felt, upholstery fabric, and drapery, do not need to be lined. Medium-weight fabrics—poplin, twill, polyester/rayon blends, and satin—are also good for backgrounds but may require lining.

All of these fabrics can be used for design elements as well. The background and elements can be the same type of material or they can be different types. Occasionally, a banner design will lend itself to the use of more unique choices: calico, terry cloth, plush felt, metallic fabrics, and taffeta.

Measure before you buy! The full-size pattern is created before the trip to the fabric store for a reason. Use a yardstick to measure the full-size pattern, then note approximately how much fabric each element will need. Running short of fabric when the banner is almost done is a hassle! Always buy extra to accommodate test gluing and coloring.

Fabrics come in widths that vary from 36″ to 60″. The width is noted on the end of the bolt. For best results, the fabric you choose for the background should be wide enough to accomodate the finished banner plus any seam allowances. In some cases, the width of your finished banner may be determined by the width of the fabric you choose for the background.

Also consider lining requirements when purchasing fabrics. Some background fabrics can be lined using fusible interfacing (available by the yard). Others can be double-layered. If the background is dark, some of the light-colored design pieces may need to be double-layered to preserve their color. Account for this when purchasing fabric. Also allow for fabric shrinkage; all washable fabrics should be preshrunk before anything is marked or cut.

Some fabrics are not suitable for banners. Knits and stretchable fabrics do not hang well and may stretch out of shape over time. Corduroy and velvet are hard to work with and can be ruined by washing and ironing.

And finally, wash and dry any washable fabrics you will be using, and iron all fabrics that can be ironed.

Choosing Colors

The wedding banner is definitely easiest to select colors for. Just ask the bride! Color choices for the rest of the banners might be more challenging.

If fabrics came only in the colors of a crayon eight-pack, explaining color choices for banners would be easy. But they do not. Fabrics are available in a huge range of colors, shades, textures, and prints. Spelling out all the possible choices for banner making would take another whole book. Instead, take a look at the colorful sample banners provided on the CD-ROM and consider the following guidelines when making color selections:

- Color is certainly a personal choice.
- Color sets the mood of the banner: vivid colors for joyful and cheerful feelings, dark colors for somber moods, pastels for peace and contentment.
- Providing contrast is a must, especially for legibility. A light background of white or pastel combined with black, dark purple, green, or blue design elements is a good choice. A dark background with light design elements also provides contrast, but remember that for full impact, light fabrics often need to be lined.
- When shopping, ask a store employee for swatches of the fabrics you are considering for letters and design elements. Unroll a yard or two of the background fabric and lay the swatches on top. Stand back and see which look best from a distance.
- For subtle variations, try using fabrics in different shades of the same color, or calico prints and solid colors in the same color family.
- Felt is very easy to work with, especially for detailed, fancy lettering. Fraying is never a worry!
- Kids love textures.
- Metallics and other shiny fabrics are great additions. They provide elegance and are surprisingly easy to work with when using iron-on fusible web.

Lessons in Lettering

Many of the banners in this book allow for personalization. Including the name of the person(s) celebrating the faith makes the banner personal and turns it into a cherished gift as well. With some simple "planning ahead" steps, adding a name and/or date to a banner is easy.

Some alphabet patterns are included on pages 92–96. It is generally best to choose a letter style that matches other letters on the banner or that provides a noticeably different style to those other letters (fig. 3).

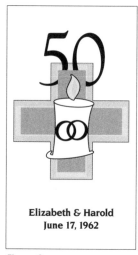 

Figure 3.

Once a letter style is selected, enlarge the chosen alphabet to the size needed. Determine the necessary size by measuring the sample name in the enlarged pattern. Follow the banner design's lead of using all capital letters or capitals and lowercase letters.

Using the photocopies, trace the words onto plain paper. Lay this tracing on the full-size banner pattern to make sure the letters fit properly. Reduce the size of the letter patterns if necessary. Keep these patterns for use with future banners.

Figure 4.

Andrew

Figure 5.

Julie

When gluing letters onto your banner, space them by eye. Do not use a ruler to measure space between letters. Imagine filling the spaces between letters with sand. Each space should get the same amount of sand (fig. 4). It is, however, a good idea to use a ruler as a baseline guide. Be aware that round letters extend a bit lower and higher than square letters (fig. 5).

Whenever working with words, always step back and check spelling and spacing before gluing!

Getting to Work

The patterns and the fabrics are ready. Finding a place to work is the next task. A large, flat spot such as a table-tennis table, dining room table, or even the kitchen floor will work. The ironing board placed next to the kitchen table and adjusted to the same height can do in a pinch (fig. 6).

Figure 6.

The Background

Before marking the fabric, make sure the paper pattern is square. A tile or linoleum floor works well because of the geometric shapes in the flooring itself. Align the pattern with the squares in the floor. Everything should be even (fig. 7). If the pattern is not square, carefully

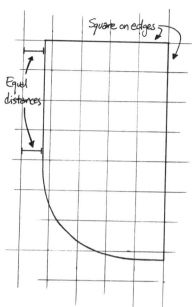

Figure 7.

trim the uneven edges. This is the best way to check banners with rounded bottoms. Another method of checking "square" is to use a tape measure. Lengths of opposite sides and diagonals should be equal (fig. 1).

Lay the fabric facedown on the work surface. Unroll the "placement pattern" facedown on top of it, and secure pattern to the fabric with a few pins. Use a pencil to mark the cut lines around the pattern, adding 3 inches to the top, 1 ½ inches to the bottom, and ½ inch to both sides. Trim the fabric along the lines.

Drape the background fabric over a rod to see how it hangs. Is it flat, or is it wavy or curling? If the fabric is sturdy and already hangs nicely, the banner will not need a lining. If the background fabric is of medium or light weight, a lining will probably make it hang much more nicely.

Unlined

Machine-stitch a ½-inch hem along both sides and a 1 ½-inch hem along the bottom. To make the top casing, lay the fabric facedown.

Mark a line 6 inches below the top edge. (Use a fabric pencil or soft lead pencil to be sure the mark does not bleed through to the right side of the fabric.) Fold down the fabric to the line and stitch. Leave the sides of the casing open to allow the hanging rod to slide through. Although strips of iron-on adhesive can be used to hem the sides and bottom, the top casing should be sewn to evenly bear the banner's weight when displayed.

Fusible Interfacing Lining

Hem the banner according to the method for unlined banners above. With the hems in place, iron fusible interfacing over the back of the entire banner. This interfacing is available by the yard in fabric stores, typically in a 22-inch width. Carefully follow manufacturer's directions provided with the interfacing and practice on scrap fabric first. When joining two pieces of interfacing, overlap them ever so slightly.

Lightweight Fabric Fusing

Measure for a top casing, but do not cut hem allowances as you will not need to sew the side or bottom hems. Cut lining fabric the same size as the banner background. (The lining can be cut from the same fabric or from a fabric of similar color.) Lay the background fabric facedown and place the lining fabric face up directly on top. Lift the edges and slide strips of iron-on fusible web between the background and lining. Iron the three layers together according to the directions for the fusible web (fig. 8). Trim uneven edges. Again, there is no need to hem the side or bottom edges, but the top casing does need to be stitched. Lay the banner facedown. Mark a line 6 inches from the top. Fold the fabric down to the line and stitch, leaving the sides open.

Machine-Stitched Lining

Cut background fabric with hem allowances, but do not sew any hems. Cut lining fabric the same size as the background. The lining can be cut from the same fabric as the background or another fabric of similar color. Pin the two pieces together with right sides facing each other. Machine-stitch the sides ½ inch from each edge. Machine-stitch across the bottom 1 ½ inches from the edge. Leave the top edge of the banner open for turning. (**Note:** If the banner is very large, it may be easier to sew side seams in two steps. After pinning background and lining, start at the middle of a side seam and sew to edge. Then sew the other half of the seam from the middle to the opposite edge. Repeat for the other side.) Turn banner right side out and press the edges. To make the top casing, lay the banner facedown and mark a line 6 inches from the top. Fold the fabric down to the line and stitch.

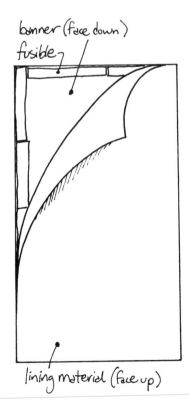

banner (face down)

fusible

lining material (face up)

Figure 8.

The Design Pieces

Cutting Out the Elements

Before cutting, write a corresponding number for each piece on the "cut-out" and the "placement" patterns. On the "cut-out" pattern, indicate the top of each piece with an arrow.

If the elements do not overlap, loosely cut around them. If they do overlap, cut the pattern pieces on the line and indicate where to add ¼ inch to the piece that goes behind. Another option is to trace another pattern to make two pieces instead of three (fig. 9).

Figure 9.

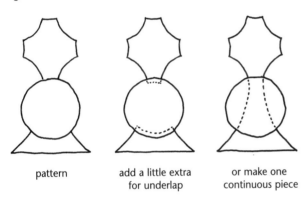

pattern   add a little extra   or make one
                 for underlap   continuous piece

Wash, dry, and iron any washable fabrics that will be used for design pieces. If the pieces will be attached with a fusible interfacing, iron it to the wrong side of the fabric according to the directions on the package.

There are two ways to go about cutting out the elements.

1. Cut out the paper pattern exactly. Lay the pattern piece facedown on the wrong side of the fabric. Using a pencil, fabric pencil, or pen, trace around the pattern onto the fabric or paper backing.

2. Loosely cut out the paper pattern. Pin the pattern to the right side of the fabric and cut pattern and fabric at the same time, cutting right on the pattern outlines. Be aware that cutting paper dulls a scissors faster than cutting fabric. A scissors that cuts both will need to be sharpened more frequently than one that cuts only fabric.

Using Fusible Interfacing for Detailed Letters

Some of the banner designs have many letters, detailed letters, or script letters. These letter styles are all ideally suited for attaching with fusible interfacing.

1. Wash, dry, and iron any washable fabrics that will be used.

2. Iron the fusible interfacing to the wrong side of the fabric, following directions on the package.

3. Pin the letter pattern, without cutting out the individual letters, to the right side of the fabric. Pin through the letters in many places to hold them securely.

4. Cut out the letters, cutting the paper pattern and the fabric at the same time.

If space is available, keep the placement pattern out for the duration of the project. As each piece is cut out, lay it in its place on the pattern to keep the elements organized. This will also help you make sure that you've cut out all the pieces needed for your banner.

Attaching the Elements

Banners put together with iron-on adhesives generally look better and work cleaner than those assembled with glue. Fusibles are slightly more expensive than glue, and some fabrics with a nap (such as corduroy and velvet) cannot take an iron and must be glued. Always test on a scrap of fabric before committing to either method!

Glue

Thick craft glue—not school glue—is best for gluing banners. Lay the background flat and arrange all the elements. Use the placement pattern as a reference. If precise placement is important, use a ruler to measure distances from the edges to the piece on the pattern, then duplicate these measurements on the banner. Begin by gluing the elements on the bottom layer. Hold down one side of the piece with a ruler; fold over the other side, smooth on a bead of glue, and return the piece to its position. Repeat with the other side of the piece. Take care to use enough glue but not so much that it bleeds through to the surface.

Fuse

When using iron-on fusible web, preparing to attach fabric is a bit more crucial than when using glue. Because you can't iron fabric when it's on the floor, it is best to set an ironing board at the same height as a large table on which the banner is lying flat. First, lay any large background pieces in place. Use a ruler as described in the previous section on gluing. Pull the banner over the ironing board section by section and iron as you go (fig. 6). When background pieces are affixed, lay the banner on the table again and arrange the remaining pieces. Repeat the process of ironing section by section, working from the bottom toward the top. Always refer to the fusible web package for instructions.

Stitch

Sewing the elements onto the banner is time consuming, but it is also the most elegant way to make a beautiful banner. It is a good idea to back each piece with fusible interfacing to prevent frayed edges.

The Finishing Touches

The details added at the end of banner making are the finishing touches that pull everything together. You can add emphasis to some design elements by outlining them with yarn, ribbon, braid, or strips of felt attached with glue. Paint is another option and can be brushed on or squeezed on. You can use a darker shade of the same color of the element to be outlined, but black is nearly always a good choice. Thin gold cord can also provide a classy finish. Use your imagination—affix buttons, sequins, or beads where you think appropriate.

Perhaps the best way to see what finishing touches are needed is to hang the banner and step back as far as possible, or lay the banner on the floor and look at it from across the room while standing on a chair. Try laying down some "finishing touches." See what looks good. But show some restraint. It can be easy to get carried away and end up with a banner that looks gaudy.

Hanging Your Work

Almost every banner is hung by a dowel rod. A ¾-inch wooden dowel is the standard. Simply slip the dowel through the banner's top casing. The banner can now be hung in several different ways.

Figure 10.

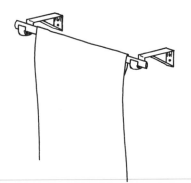

Figure 11.

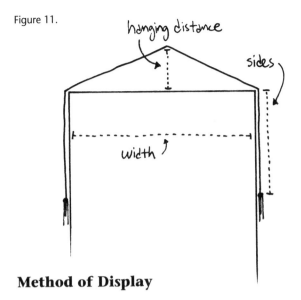

Method of Display

1. From the Wall

Securely mount two appropriately sized curtain rod hooks to the wall. Set the banner's dowel rod in the hooks. The hooks are permanent and can be used again (fig. 10).

2. From the Ceiling

Find a brave soul to climb to the ceiling to attach two lengths of 15 lb. test fishing line. Tie an S hook at the end of each line that can accommodate the banner's dowel rod. These lines can also be permanent and will very rarely be noticed, even without a banner hanging from them. Be sure that both lines are the same length so the banner will hang level.

3. With a Rope or Cord

This is probably the most common and most versatile method for hanging a banner. Many types of cord are available at fabric stores. Browse the bolts and select one that complements the banner. Often white or gold is the best choice. Purchase enough to accommodate the width of the banner plus hanging distance plus any length wanted down the sides (fig. 11).

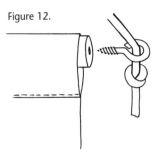

Figure 12.

Before you slide the dowel through the casing, attach an eye screw at each end of the dowel. Thread the cord through each eye screw and knot the cord at the point where it should hang (fig. 12). The banner can now be hung on a banner pole or from a hook in the wall.

To prevent the banner from shifting (especially for processional banners), tie one overhand knot in the middle of the cord. Hang the loop on the pole's hook.

Making a Pole Stand

If no banner pole stand is available, some basic carpentry skills and the following diagram will provide a durable, functional stand (fig. 13). The base should measure 18 x 18 inches square. The center square that holds the pole should be 18 inches tall.

The pole itself can be wood, metal, or PVC. A hook from which the banner will be hung should be fastened to the top.

Figure 13.

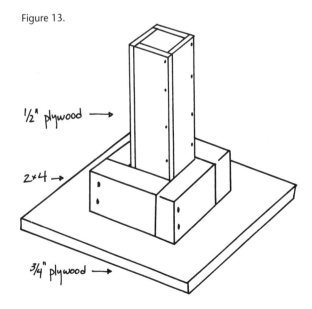

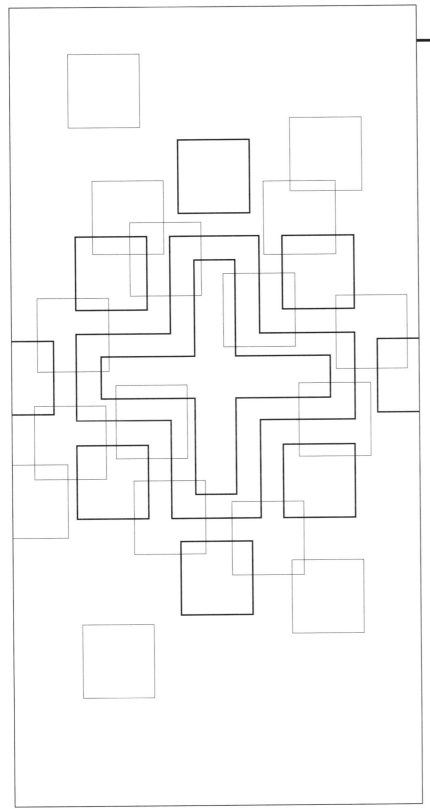

Tips & Extras ..·········...

- The squares and cross icon (as separated, below) should stand out the most and be made from one color. With a white background, make the icon from gold lamé. On a dark background, make the icon gold or white.

- For the remaining squares, choose colors that stand out from the background and complement one another.

- The remaining squares could be layered cotton fabric or felt. The squares and cross icon should be the topmost layer. Consider outlining on the gold fabric where the squares underlap the icon cross/squares. Use ribbon, yarn or squeeze paint.

- Or, for a stained glass look, layer translucent fabrics, such as chiffon or organza. These fabrics could layer above or below the gold cross icon. Use more than one thickness of these fabrics to vary the color and shade. Attach to the banner with tacky glue or hot glue just at the corners of each square, or sew them on, stitching 1 inch from the edge of the square and leaving an unfinished edge to give the banner texture.

Cross

Declare His glory among the nations, His marvelous works among all the peoples! Psalm 96:3

Tips & Extras......................

- Make a fabric earth, starting with a blue circle. Then glue on the green or brown land shapes. Paint the globe lines using quick strokes and wispy marks. (Practice on scrap fabric first!) Next, add the cross icon using a bright, contrasting fabric (white, yellow-orange, gold, or silver). If necessary, outline the cross icon with paint or cord to help it stand out.

- For a more artistic look, paint the water and land using watercolor paint and big, bold strokes. Don't feel compelled to fill it all in— let some background show. After the paint dries, add the fabric cross icon. Finish the globe lines with paint or yarn.

- This would be a great banner for a Mission Sunday or outreach program.

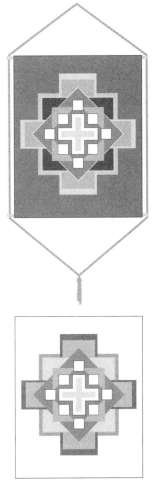

Tips & Extras

- Make this a quilt-inspired banner by using solids, stripes, prints, and calicos in any number of color palettes.

- Or use a subtle color scheme of black, silver, gray, and white. Emphasize the cross icon with a bit of color.

- Put this design on a background of any shape: a processional banner, a very tall banner for display in the chancel or a stairwell, or even a round banner! Cut the fabric several inches larger than finished size, wrap the edges around plywood cut to size, and use a staple gun to attach. Use eye screws and picture-frame wire to hang.

Tips & Extras..............

- For a light color scheme, make the background white and the three-bubble element silver. The three cross icons should all be the same: a dark color for the squares, the cross the same dark color with a silver center outlined with black trim.

- In reverse, make the background a dark color and the three-bubble element a similar dark color (navy blue and purple, black and burgundy). Make the cross icons silver or gold with the cross centers white.

- Looking for a processional banner challenge? Consider creating one that will allow light to show through for a great, unique look. Start with transparent chiffon fabric the size of the entire banner. This fabric will eventually make up the three-bubble element. Next, choose fabric for the left and right sides of the banner. You will need to have two of each side—one each for the banner front and back. Line this fabric with fusible web, then cut out the four pieces. Now make a sandwich: left side and right side facing down, chiffon rectangle, left side and right side facing up. Finally, attach six "squares and cross" icons, three on the front of the banner and three on the back. This banner will be seen from front and back.

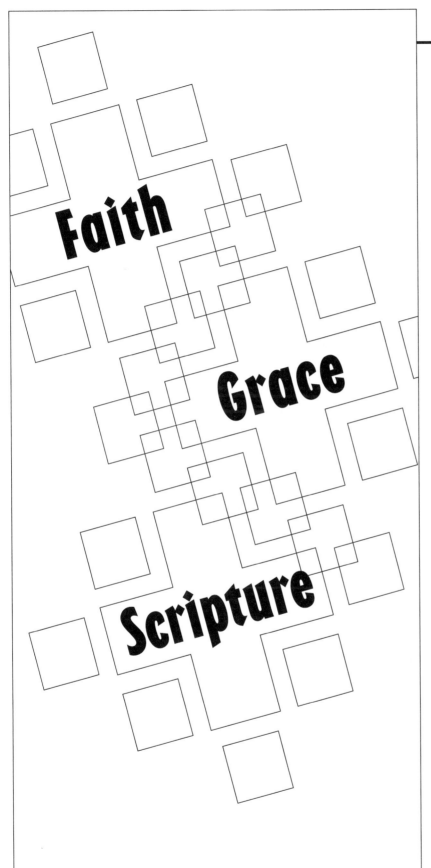

Tips & Extras········ ·········

- This banner visually depicts how faith, grace, and Scripture are all connected.

- Read "Tips & Extras" for the cross design on page 17 for suggestions on making this banner full of squares.

- The words should be cut from a fabric that contrasts sharply with the cross fabric.

Cross

Tips & Extras

• This banner is well suited for an entryway. It would also make a great floor painting or mosaic in a church foyer.

• Try a mosaic banner: Choose a heavier background fabric such as twill or canvas. Using a pencil, lightly trace the design outline onto the background, not including the eight squares and cross icon. Select a fabric to fill each of the four areas: center circle, four-point star, twelve-point star, and outer circle. Cut many small (approximately 3/4-inch) squares from these fabrics. Arrange the small squares on your background neatly or randomly, whichever you prefer. Some background should show between the little squares. Don't worry too much about staying exactly within the pencil lines. Attach the small squares using hot glue, tacky glue, or fusible web. Select a contrasting fabric for the eight squares and cross—perhaps gold lamé or bright white outlined with shiny gold braid. Affix over the top of the mosaic pieces. Add the small circle pieces; consider using jewels.

• Use trim (cord, braid, sequins, etc.) to embellish. Remember that the banner will most likely be viewed from a distance, so use trim thick enough to be seen.

Cross

"I am the Alpha and the Omega, the first and the last, the beginning and the end." Revelation 22:13

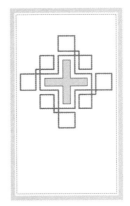 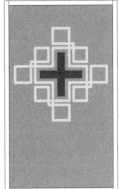

Tips & Extras················

- The squares on this banner are made from a continuous line.

- Consider using a translucent background fabric that can be seen through when the finished banner hangs. Easily transfer the design onto the background by laying a full-size pattern under the background fabric and tracing.

- Use braided cord or ribbon for the continuous line; quality fabric stores will have hundreds to choose from! Cord and ribbon can be difficult to attach. Experiment with scraps using thick craft glue, hot glue, or fusible web.

- Make the center of the cross using the same cord, or make it from a complementary fabric.

- If you use fabric for the cross center, consider using the same fabric for a border. Make the border as wide or narrow as you like.

Cross

With my whole heart I seek You;
let me not wander from Your
commandments! Psalm 119:10

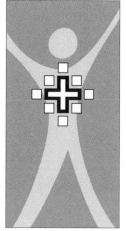 

Tips & Extras . . . .

- Use spray paint for the person shape and background: Cut a full-size paper pattern of the person. Use a light coat of spray adhesive to attach it to the background fabric. Spray-paint the background, then remove the paper pattern. Experiment with scraps first, varying the coverage amount. Lighter to darker and fine mist to coarse spray add visual interest.

- If spray paint isn't your thing, try patterned fabrics for added visual interest.

- The cross and squares should contrast with the background and person. Outline in black or gold trim to accentuate the contrast.

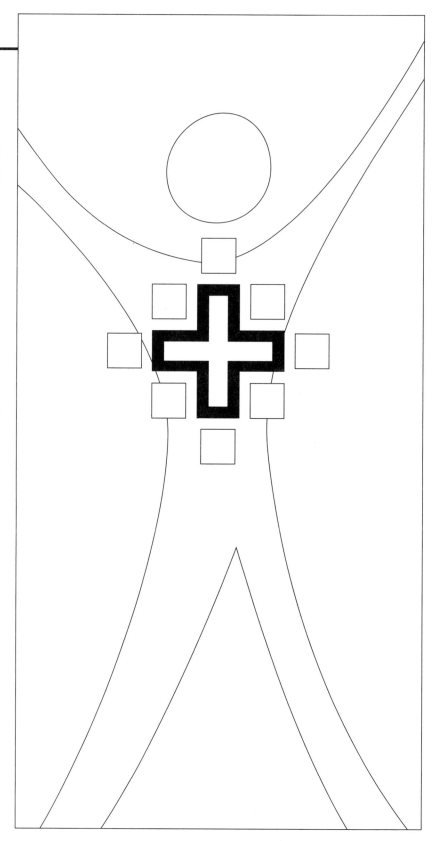

Cross

Tips & Extras . . . .

- The spiral in this design visually represents the concept that for Christians, it all comes down to the cross.

- Accentuate this spiral by using wide, flat braid in contrast with the background, or downplay the spiral by using a lighter or darker shade of the background fabric.

- The cross itself should stand out more than the spiral.

- Trim the squares and cross with cord half as wide as that used for the spiral.

Cross

Tips & Extras·····················

- Sometimes the simplest banners can become the most elegant. Select a background fabric with inlaid pattern. Use shiny satin or several layers of "sparkle" organza for the cross and squares. If using a translucent fabric like organza, tack it to the banner with craft glue or a hot-glue gun just at the corners of each square. You may also sew the fabric in place, stitching 1 inch from the edges of the square and leaving an unfinished edge to give the banner some texture.

- Leave out the background "sweep" for a simpler, more symmetrical banner.

- Trim with coordinating rattail or other narrow cord.

Proclaim His Death

Service of the Sacrament

Divine Service, Setting 1

*For as often as you eat this bread
and drink the cup, you proclaim
the Lord's death until He comes.
1 Corinthians 11:26*

Proclaim His Death

Tips & Extras . . . .

• Using shiny fabric for grapes and wheat would help them stand out from the cross.

• View your "in progress" banner from a distance. Outline elements as you think necessary.

• Omit the words for a simpler construction.

Divine Service, Setting 2

And He took bread, and when He had given thanks, He broke it and gave it to them, saying, "This is My body, which is given for you. Do this in remembrance of Me." Luke 22:19

Tips & Extras········

• This could be a two-color banner by using one color fabric for the background and a second for the image and words.

• When making a multicolored banner, build it in layers. Using fusible web, attach a solid fabric circle to the background. Then attach grapes, leaves, and four quarter-circle shapes. Be careful not to fuse the overhanging edge of the circle to your ironing board.

• Use fusible interfacing to line the back of the banner so the fabric does not droop where the circle overhangs the background.

• For a pastel color scheme, use a background of pastel purple, black icon, pastel purple and green for the grapes and leaves, and white for the quarters of the circle.

THIS DO

IN REMEMBRANCE OF ME

Divine Service, Setting 3

The next day he saw Jesus coming toward him, and said, "Behold, the Lamb of God, who takes away the sin of the world!" John 1:29

Tips & Extras.............

- Work in layers. Using fusible web, attach one big shape of the cross and lamb to the background. Next, fuse the cross pieces and lamb onto the big shape. (See below.)

- Add dimension by trimming the lamb shapes and lamb outline in gold cord.

- The Scripture reference could be cut from fabric, spelled out with the trim cord, or painted.

John 1:29

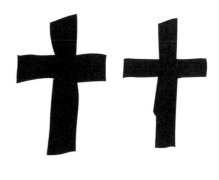

Divine Service, Setting 4

And He took bread, and when He had given thanks, He broke it and gave it to them, saying, "This is My body, which is given for you. Do this in remembrance of Me." Luke 22:19

Tips & Extras . . . .

• Make the background a cream color; make the oval shape the same color, but use a shiny fabric.

• For best results, follow the instructions for detailed letters on page 12.

Now as they were eating, Jesus took bread, and after blessing it broke it and gave it to the disciples, and said, "Take, eat; this is My body." And He took a cup, and when He had given thanks He gave it to them, saying, "Drink of it, all of you, for this is My blood of the covenant, which is poured out for many for the forgiveness of sins."
Matthew 26:26–29

Tips & Extras

• A dark blue background with metallic brass cross, gold burst, and silver challis would make a striking banner. Finish by trimming all the elements with white cord.

• Consider using a white background with the same metallic fabric elements trimmed with thick black cord or several rounds of yarn.

• To eliminate the need for trimming with cord, make this banner in layers on one big background shape. (See below.) Using fusible web, first iron the big background shape onto your banner rectangle. Then fuse the arms of the cross, the burst triangles, and the three challis pieces to the background shape. Done!

Matins

O Lord, our Lord, how majestic is Your name in all the earth! Psalm 8:1

Tips & Extras

- The background and fabric for "Lord Jesus" should be similar in value, both being lighter shades or darker shades. "IHS" should stand out the most. For example, make a navy blue "IHS" on white background with tan "Lord Jesus," or gold "IHS" trimmed in white on dark green background with dark blue "Lord Jesus."

- The bottom edge of the banner can be cut to any shape you like. The rounded edge seems to suit this design and could be dressed up with a row of string fringe or beaded fringe. Fringe can be sewn on or attached with a hot-glue gun. Fusible web is not recommended for attaching fringe or braid.

- Use a rod that extends past the edge of the banner by 6 inches on both sides. Leave long ends on the hanging cord and add tassels for a decorative finish.

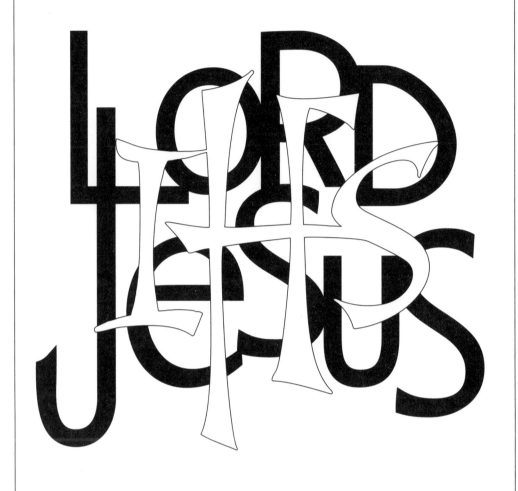

The steadfast love of the LORD never ceases; His mercies never come to an end; they are new every morning; great is Your faithfulness. Lamentations 3:22–23

Tips & Extras

• Try using bright blue spray paint on the "sky" area before attaching any other pieces. Hold the can 12–18 inches above the fabric and mist with color. Fade from almost white near the horizon to mostly blue at the top. Practice on newspaper first.

• Use a patterned or calico shade of green for the bottom half of the banner.

• Make the sun yellow. The sun's outline and rays should be a bright yellow-orange.

• Be sure the color of your letters stands out from the green fabric. For best results, follow the instructions for detailed letters on page 12.

Vespers

*"I am the Alpha and the Omega," says
the Lord God, "who is and who was
and who is to come, the Almighty."
Revelation 1:8*

Tips & Extras..·····..........

- These banners work as a pair. Display them
  on both sides of the chancel, both sides of the
  sanctuary, on either side of entry doors, and
  so on.

- Make the half-circles and the borders from
  yellows and oranges; contrast the A and Ω by
  making them a dark color like purple or dark
  green.

- The two banners could have matching color
  schemes. Or, make them with opposite color
  schemes: light colors on dark for one banner,
  dark colors on light for the other.

Evening Prayer

For God, who said, "Let light shine out of darkness," made His light shine in our hearts to give us the light of the knowledge of the glory of God in the face of Christ. 2 Corinthians 4:6 NIV

Tips & Extras............

- Build this banner in layers with striking color choices. Begin with a tan background, add a white cross, then add a silver 8-pointed star. For the final layer, add the gold four-pointed star and four gold triangles. (See below.)

- For a bolder look, use a purple or burgundy background with white cross, black eight-pointed star, and silver and gold four-pointed stars.

- Finish with black squeeze paint to outline all elements.

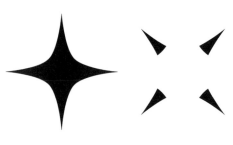

It is good to give thanks to the Lord, to sing praises to Your name, O Most High; to declare Your steadfast love in the morning, and Your faithfulness by night. Psalm 92:1–2

Tips & Extras ·············

- Make the Bible black and white, the candle red, and the flame yellow with an orange center. The background could be white and the letters dark purple or blue.

- Trim the flame in yellow eyelash yarn to give it "flicker." Hang yellow fringe from the bottom of the banner to balance the colors.

Prayer and Preaching

"Behold, God is my salvation; I will trust, and will not be afraid; for the LORD GOD is my strength and my song, and He has become my salvation."
Isaiah 12:2

Tips & Extras..............

- This banner is a picture of the cross of Jesus bringing out the sun from behind a storm cloud.

- One color scheme possibility is a dark gray cloud, medium brown cross, yellow sun with yellow-orange rays, light blue sky, black Bible with white pages, and red nails to represent Christ's blood.

- There are many other color options for this banner. Make several photocopies of the small-size pattern and use markers or crayons to experiment with color schemes.

- Consider using paint instead of fabric to highlight the edges of the cloud and make the sun's rays. Use diluted acrylic paint, a wide sponge brush, and sweeping strokes. Practice on scraps first, and don't worry about following the pattern exactly! If your background fabric is translucent enough, color the sun's rays in black on your full-size pattern, then put the pattern under the fabric, and use it as a guide when painting.

Responsive Prayer

Let my prayer be counted as incense before You, and the lifting up of my hands as the evening sacrifice! Psalm 141:2

Tips & Extras......

- The background shapes of this design depict a flame and rising smoke.

- Background suggestion A: Make the flame out of metallic or sparkly fabric. Use light to medium shades of gray ribbon or yarn for the "smoke" lines.

- Background suggestion B: Create the smoke feel with dark gray and/or black spray paint. Using a pencil, lightly trace the smoke lines from the pattern onto your background fabric. Lay the fabric out in the yard. Holding the can 12 inches above the fabric, spray in long sweeps. Spray paint allows you to make darker and lighter lines that blend into each other and the background. The softness of the background smoke will contrast nicely with the sharpness of the cross and candle. Practice on newspaper first!

Note: *Before spraying the entire background, check to see if your large flame fabric is opaque enough to cover the smoke. If it is not, mask the large flame on the background with a paper cutout temporarily taped in place.*

- The background cross can be any dark color. Make a white candle, black cross, and yellow-orange flame. The candle especially should be outlined. Either use black cord or layer fabrics to create a black edge: a large black shape first with two white candle pieces on top.

Brief Service of the Word

"For God so loved the world, that He gave His only Son, that whoever believes in Him should not perish but have eternal life." John 3:16

Tips & Extras........

- Suggestion A: white background, tan large cross, gold smaller cross, black Bible cover, shiny white pages.
- Suggestion B: background in a medium shade, flat white large cross, gold smaller cross, black Bible cover, shiny white pages.
- Trim the crosses with flat braid or cord to dress up this banner.

Baptism

"Therefore go and make disciples of all nations, baptizing them in the name of the Father and of the Son and of the Holy Spirit, and teaching them to obey everything I have commanded you." Matthew 28:19–20 NIV

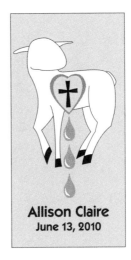
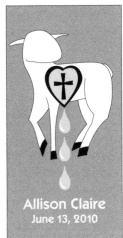

Tips & Extras

- Make this banner as a gift for a godchild, grandchild, niece, or nephew. Personalize it by adding the child's name and Baptism date at the bottom. For best results, follow the instructions for detailed letters on page 12.

- Make the banner in a smaller size (approximately 18 x 32 inches) so it can be displayed in the child's room after the service.

- Vary the textures of the fabrics. A young child will love to feel the differences! Make the lamb from fleece or simulated lamb's-wool fabric, the heart and hooves from vinyl, and the water droplets from something sparkly and rough.

- If you use a wooly fabric for the lamb, cut the fabric away from where the heart will be rather than trying to glue or sew the heart on top of the wool. Plan to outline the lamb with black paint or cord.

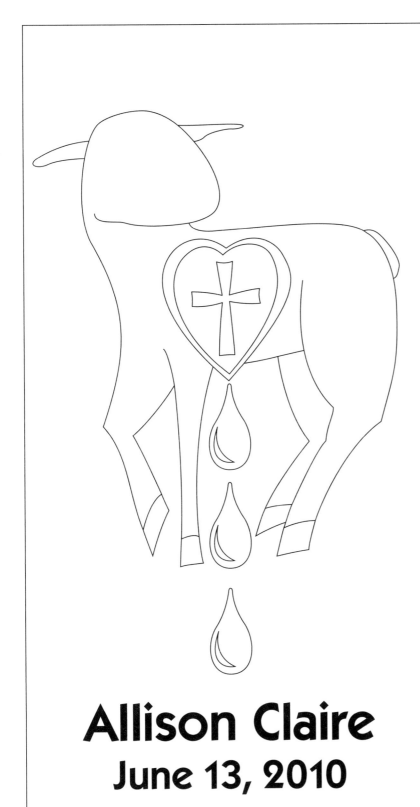

Allison Claire
June 13, 2010

Baptism

*Rise and be baptized and wash away
your sins, calling on His name.
Acts 22:16*

Tips & Extras.........

- The background rays symbolize the coming of the Holy Spirit. Make them gold lamé or shiny satin.

- Layer the shell, starting with a larger black or dark blue shell shape, then adding the smaller white shell shape.

- Or cut out only the smaller shell shape. Affix it to the background and rays, then add the shell details, and outline with cord or paint.

- The top piece of this banner is intended to be permanently hung in the church near the baptismal font. The bottom piece is to be made as a personalized banner for each newly baptized person. For best results, follow the instructions for detailed letters on page 12.

- The top banner should have a casing and dowel rod at the top *and* bottom. The smaller banner needs a casing and dowel rod at the top with a thin cord for hanging it at home. During the service, hang the small, personalized banner from the bottom of the large banner. Use loops made from the same cord that hangs the large banner, or use several links of chain.

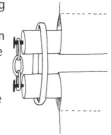

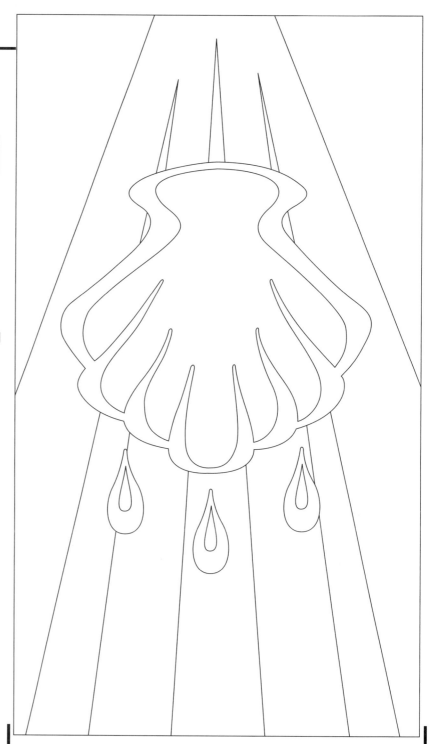

JACOB CHARLES

FEB. 7   2012

+

John Andrew
8·13·2010

Jesus answered, "Truly, truly I say to you, unless one is born of water and the Spirit, he cannot enter the kingdom of God." John 3:5

Tips & Extras · · · · · · · · · · · · · · ·

• The background should be white. Make the rays from gold lamé, or use lengths of gold braid. The dove should be layered: shiny white fabric on black fabric.

• Suggestion A for the water: Use metallic or sequined fabric to give the water "shimmer," then glue white swirls on top for the three waves.

• Suggestion B: Use regular fabric of a medium blue shade; add thick lines of blue glitter paint for the three swirls.

• Suggestion C: Use regular blue fabric for the water and regular light blue fabric for the swirls. Nobody said it has to sparkle!

• Personalize this banner by adding a name and Baptism date. For best results, follow the instructions for detailed letters on page 12.

Baptism

But you were washed, you were sanctified, you were justified in the name of the Lord Jesus Christ and by the Spirit of our God. 1 Corinthians 6:11

Tips & Extras . . . .

• See Tips & Extras from the banner on page 42.

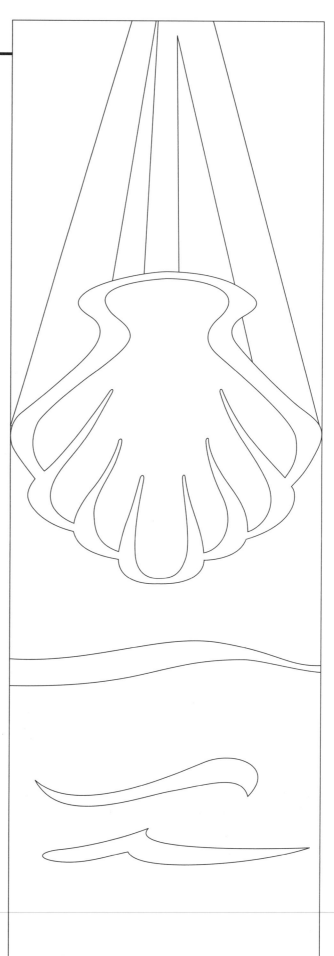

Anna Kate
May 8, 2010

Whoever believes and is baptized will be saved. Mark 16:16

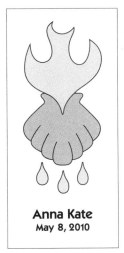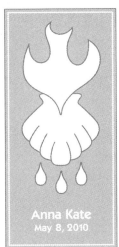

Anna Kate
May 8, 2010

Tips & Extras ·····

- To a dark blue background, add a white dove, an off-white shell, and light blue water droplets. Outline as you see fit.

- Consider using small-patterned fabrics for all the elements.

- Personalize this banner as a gift for a godchild, grandchild, niece, or nephew by adding the child's name and Baptism date at the bottom. For best results, follow the instructions for detailed letters on page 12. Make the banner a smaller size (18 x 32 inches) so it can be displayed in the child's room after the service.

Confirmation

Whoever confesses Me before men, him I will also confess before My Father who is in heaven. But whoever denies Me before men, him I will also deny before My Father who is in heaven. Matthew 10:32—33 NKJV

Tips & Extras

- Make the background off-white so the white dove and Bible stand out.

- For easy construction, layer the five shapes as indicated below. Outline crosses as you see fit.

- Include a list of the confirmands' names by using cutout letters or writing them with squeeze paint. If painting, ensure straight lines, neat letters, and correct spelling by printing the names from a computer at full size. Lay this paper under the fabric and trace the names. If you cannot see through the fabric, tape the paper to a large, sunny window, tape the fabric over the paper, and then trace with a pencil. Lay the banner on a table when painting the names. If you use the window method, paint the names before attaching the symbols.

- Display the banner for some time after the confirmation service, perhaps in the church entryway, to encourage and remind the congregation to keep the confirmands in their prayers.

ANDREW DAVID

LAUREN MICHELLE

ELLIE FAITH

RUTH MARIE

AMY ANNETTE

JOSHUA MICHAEL

EVAN K.

KELLY ALICE

To Him [Jesus] all the prophets bear witness that everyone who believes in Him receives forgiveness of sins through His name. Acts 10:43

Tips & Extras ·····················

- Make the background red, the dove metallic silver lamé, and the shell/Bible/chalice white with black outlines.

- To make the outlines, use a thick bead of black squeeze paint. Or, using iron-on fusible web, layer white shell/Bible/chalice shapes onto one slightly larger black shape. (See below.)

- Make the rays using gold braid or cord.

Confirmation

You, however, are not in the flesh but in the Spirit, if in fact the Spirit of God dwells in you. Romans 8:9

Tips & Extras . . . .

- The world image behind the dove could be made from blue fabric with green fabric for the land areas, or cut a single circle from fabric that has blues and greens in it. Make the banner's border blue or use the blue/green fabric.

- Cut one piece of black fabric that will be the dove outline and the person. Affix the four white shapes that will make the dove in layers.

- Add the words in the same green fabric used for the land, or use blue fabric that coordinates with the blue/green fabric of the world.

- Omit the words if you think the visual elements speak for themselves, or add only the Scripture reference.

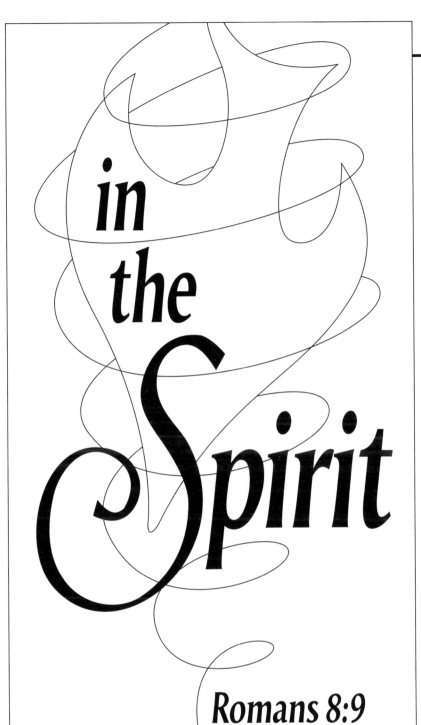

in the Spirit

Romans 8:9

You, however, are not in the flesh but in the Spirit, if in fact the Spirit of God dwells in you. Romans 8:9

Tips & Extras⋯⋯⋯⋯⋯

- Color scheme A: gold background (metallic or felt), white dove, and red letters. Use black cord or paint for the spiral, taking care to give the illusion of going around (in front of and behind) the words too.

- Color scheme B: red background, white dove, black letters, and a shiny gold spiral.

- A gold hanging cord with tassels down the side would complement the gold dove or spiral.

- Include or delete the Scripture reference as you see fit.

Holy Matrimony

Therefore a man shall leave his father and his mother and hold fast to his wife, and they shall become one flesh.
Genesis 2:24

Tips & Extras . . . .

- Color scheme A: white background; gold lamé background cross; Chi-Rho, border and "one" a dark color, perhaps matching the bridesmaids' dresses.

- Color scheme B: white twill for the background; satin or other shiny, patterned white for the background cross. The Chi-Rho should be the wedding party's color, and "one" will be gold lamé.

- The border could be a simple band of the wedding color; or experiment with cords, ribbons, braids, or fabric in the wedding color and gold.

- Make a beautiful wedding gift by adding the couple's names and wedding date at the bottom. For best results, follow the instructions for detailed letters on page 12.

Love
as
Christ
loved us.

James & Megan
May 24, 2009

Therefore be imitators of God, as beloved children. And walk in love, as Christ loved us and gave Himself up for us, a fragrant offering and sacrifice to God. Ephesians 5:1–2

Tips & Extras

- These letters are not going to be easy to cut out, but the result will be beautiful! The best way to work with detailed letters like these is to follow the instructions for detailed letters found on page 12.
- Use wide gold ribbon to quickly make a cross and border. If the ribbon has wire in the edges, pull the wire out before affixing the ribbon to the banner.
- Make the wedding rings from gold lamé. Use fusible web to prevent fraying.
- Include the couple's names and wedding date at the bottom to make a beautiful, personal addition to the ceremony.

Holy Matrimony

Therefore be imitators of God, as beloved children. And walk in love, as Christ loved us and gave Himself up for us, a fragrant offering and sacrifice to God. Ephesians 5:1–2

Tips & Extras

- Use a dark color for the letters. For best results, follow the instructions for detailed letters on page 12.
- Make the cross and rings in a coordinating lighter color or gold.
- Instead of a trim border, try a fancy fringe along the bottom and tassels from the hanging rod for an elegant finish.

Michael & Amy
June 4, 2009

United
in Christ

May 24, 2012

May the God of endurance and encouragement grant you to live in such harmony with one another, in accord with Christ Jesus, that together you may with one voice glorify the God and Father of our Lord Jesus Christ.
Romans 15:5–6

Tips & Extras

• Make the wedding cross from silver or gold lamé. Use fusible web to prevent fraying.

• Use a dark color for the letters. For best results, follow the instructions for detailed letters on page 12.

• The border could be a simple band of the wedding color, or experiment with cords, ribbons, braids, or fabric in the wedding color and gold.

• Make a beautiful wedding gift by adding the couple's names and wedding date at the bottom. The banner will be a great reminder of God's presence in the couple's marriage and home.

• Make coordinating altar and pulpit paraments using the same color scheme as the banner and omitting the words. Consult your pastor before starting.

Holy Matrimony

Though a man might prevail against one who is alone, two will withstand him—a threefold cord is not quickly broken. Ecclesiastes 4:12

Tips & Extras

- A one-color background fabric with an inlaid pattern would be a good choice.
- *Many* color schemes would work for this banner. Start with wedding party colors, gold, white, and black. Experiment! Photocopy the pattern and try different color combinations using markers or colored pencils. Be sure the wedding rings/cross and its outline fabric stand out the most.
- Explore shiny and dull fabrics in the same color family.
- Trim with flat braid to highlight a layer that needs more emphasis.

Joseph & Kate
September 28, 2009

1 Corinthians 15

When the perishable puts on the imperishable, and the mortal puts on immortality, then shall come to pass the saying that is written: "Death is swallowed up in victory." "O death, where is your victory? O death, where is your sting?" The sting of death is sin, and the power of sin is the law. But thanks be to God, who gives us the victory through our Lord Jesus Christ.
1 Corinthians 15:54–57

Tips & Extras········ ········

• Instead of making the cross from fabric, use ribbon to outline the cross shape. Consider also using cord in a lighter shade of the same color used for "Victory." This would look nice on a white background with a gold Jesus figure and a dark color for "Victory."

• A second color scheme: light background (light blue), gold cross, white Jesus figure, and dark word (purple). Look at the banner from a distance; would the banner look better if the cross were outlined with white? purple? or not at all?

• Include or omit the Scripture reference at your discretion.

• Speak with your pastor about the possibility of using the funeral banner in the procession into church before the service.

Funeral

When the perishable puts on the imperishable, and the mortal puts on immortality, then shall come to pass the saying that is written: "Death is swallowed up in victory." "O death, where is your victory? O death, where is your sting?" The sting of death is sin, and the power of sin is the law. But thanks be to God, who gives us the victory through our Lord Jesus Christ. 1 Corinthians 15:54–57

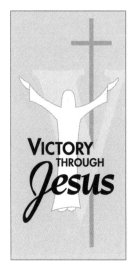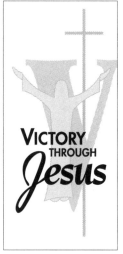

Tips & Extras

- At the fabric store, experiment with different combinations of off-white, tan, and white for the background, *V*, and Jesus figure. The cross and letters should be a dark color so they are easy to read.

- For best results, follow the instructions for detailed letters on page 12.

- The cross can be made quickly by using wide ribbon.

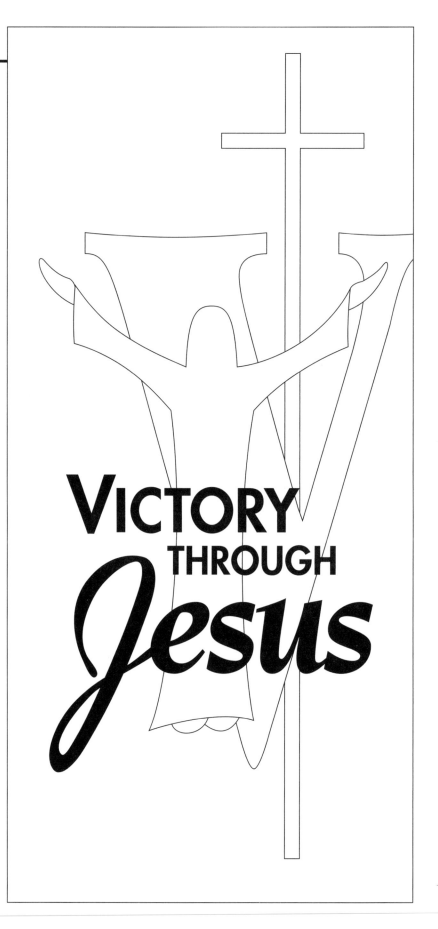

And when the Chief Shepherd appears, you will receive the crown of glory that will never fade away. 1 Peter 5:4 NIV

Tips & Extras·············

• Make the crown from gold and silver lamé. Add detail with jewels or sequined trim.

• For best results, follow the instructions for detailed letters on page 12.

• Add fringe along the bottom edge to visually balance the banner. Use fringe in the same color as the crown.

Funeral

"I am the resurrection and the life. He who believes in Me will live, even though he dies; and whoever lives and believes in Me will never die."
John 11:25–26 NIV

Tips & Extras

- Use fabric with a green, leafy print for the stem and leaves.

- Make the bloom from shiny satin fabric.

- If both the background and the bloom are white, layer the bloom and leaves over black for a wide black outline.

- The rectangles at the top and bottom could be the same color as the leaves
or the same color as the letters.

- For best results, follow the instructions for detailed letters on page 12.

- Display the banner with a row of potted lilies in front and/or at the sides.

Who ever believes in ME though he die, yet shall he LIVE

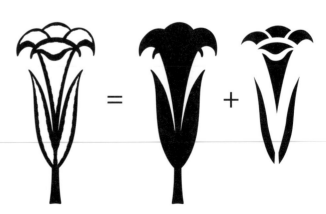

to such belongs the **Kingdom** of **God**

And they were bringing children to Him that He might touch them, and the disciples rebuked them. But when Jesus saw it, He was indignant and said to them, "Let the children come to Me; do not hinder them, for to such belongs the kingdom of God." Mark 10:13–14

Tips & Extras

- When the background is white, paint the lines of the lamb's legs and the hand's fingers black. Also outline the shapes in black.

- When using a dark background fabric, the lines making the fingers can be made with thin strips of the background fabric.

- Use ribbon to make the cross.

- On a white background, the letters can be any dark color.

Pastor

Jesus said to Simon Peter, "Simon, son of John, do you love Me more than these?" He said to him, "Yes, Lord; You know that I love You." He said to him, "Feed My lambs." John 21:15

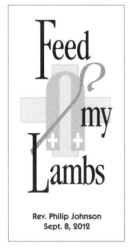

Tips & Extras

- When choosing colors for the cross, stole, and staff, take care to coordinate them so each element can be recognized from a distance.

- For best results, follow the instructions for detailed letters on page 12.

- Help your congregation's new pastor feel welcome by making this banner as a gift to him. Personalize by adding his name and installation date at the bottom.

Vicar

Having gifts...

...Let us use them.

Romans 12

Having gifts that differ according to the grace given to us, let us use them.
Romans 12:6

Tips & Extras · · · · · · · · · · · · · · ·

• The burst shape should be subtle in appearance. Make it and the background from similar colors.

• Consider using spray paint on the background fabric to make the burst. Cut an actual size burst shape out of paper. Use a light coat of spray adhesive to temporarily attach this paper mask to the background fabric. With spray paint, create a fade of color that seems to radiate from the center of the burst. Remove the paper mask after the paint dries.

• With a light background, consider making the lamp and Bible all silver with black trim. Satin or other shiny fabric would look great. Trim with paint or cord, or layer two colors of fabric. (See below.)

• For best results, follow the instructions for detailed letters on page 12.

• If the burst looks like too much work, just leave it off!

Church Worker

For the one who sows to his own flesh will from the flesh reap corruption, but the one who sows to the Spirit will from the Spirit reap eternal life. And let us not grow weary of doing good, for in due season we will reap, if we do not give up. Galatians 6:8–9

Tips & Extras

• The fish and cross in the banner are meant to be secondary to the words. Use muted colors like shiny gray or tan for the fish, shiny brown or black for the cross. Outline and detail the fish with black.

• Choose bright fabric for the letters. You can't go wrong with letters all the same color, or try four different colors: 1) Sow, 2) to the, 3) Spirit, 4) Galatians 6.

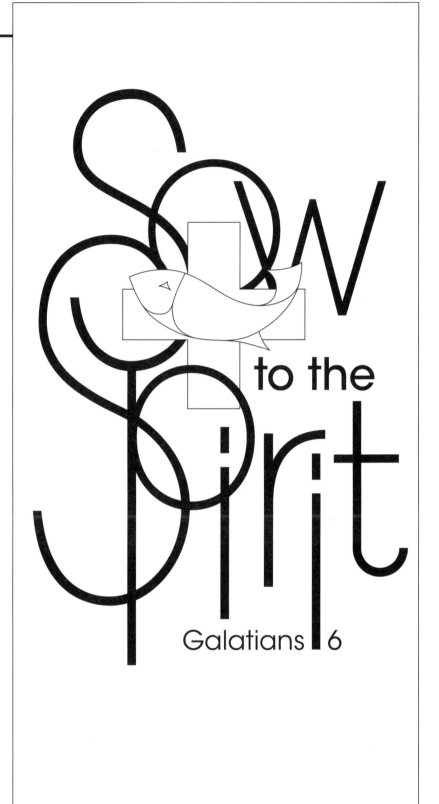

Day School Teacher

Let the word of Christ dwell in you richly, teaching and admonishing one another in all wisdom . . . with all thankfulness to God. Colossians 3:16

Tips & Extras

- Try making the background of this banner from semi-sheer fabrics like chiffon or organza. Don't line this fabric. Start with a full square of color A for the background. Sew on the tall, capital "I" shape from color B, or simply another layer or two of color A. The final sewn-on translucent shape will be the large circle. Again, choose a different color or additional layers of one used already. Now sew the top casing, doubling over the fabric since it is very thin. Sew a casing along the bottom edge as well and add a dowel rod so the fabric hangs taut and straight. For the rest of the banner, use opaque fabrics.

- Add a thin band around the circle using cord or flat braid.

- Display this banner when a new day school teacher is installed or each year when the school year begins.

A

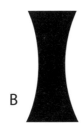

B

C

Sunday School Teacher

Love the Lord *your God with all your heart ... Teach (these words) diligently to your children. Deuteronomy 6:5–7*

Tips & Extras............

- Don't feel obligated to use red just because the shape is a heart. A good choice would be to use white or off-white for the center of the heart and two darker or brighter colors for the background and heart outline.

- Make the clothes different colors but all of the same value. They should coordinate with your color choice for the background.

- When making the faces, use colors of fabric that reflect the ethnicity of your Sunday School.

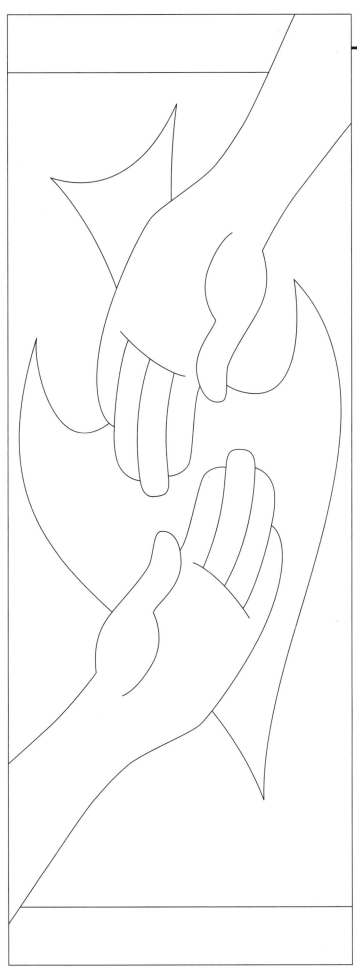

Servants

As each has received a gift, use it to serve one another ... whoever serves, as one who serves by the strength that God supplies. 1 Peter 4:10–11

Tips & Extras ···········

- The hands in this banner represent two relationships: God strengthening man and man serving man.
- Make the dove from fabric, or only outline the dove shape using cord.
- Be sure the hands contrast with the background and the dove. Use black to outline the hands and form the fingers and thumb.
- Display this banner when church officers and board or committee members are installed, before your congregation sends youth group members on a servant event, or during a time when the congregation or the community at large is in need.

Pastor

To You, the Counselor, we cry,
To You, the gift of God Most High;
The fount of life, the fire of love,
The soul's anointing from above.
(LSB 498)

Tips & Extras········

- The color of the day for an ordination service is red. The background and stole on this banner should be red.

- Cut out the flames from white cotton fabric. Color each flame yellow and orange with washable markers, then drip water onto the flames to blend the colors together. Or use watercolor paints and blend for a similar look.

- The small dove and flames should be outlined or layered onto a darker color to help them stand out. Black always works; here consider using orange or red. (See lower right for layering patterns.)

Commit your way to the LORD; trust in Him and He will act. Psalm 37:5

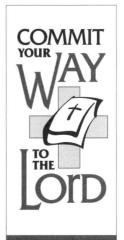

Tips & Extras . . . .

• For the Bible, layer white on black fabric. (See below for layering patterns.)

• The rest of the elements can be any combination of colors that appeals to you. Be sure the letters and background contrast enough to be seen from a distance. Letters could be all one color; or make "Way" and "Lord" one color, the rest of the words another. For best results in attaching the letters, follow the instructions on page 12.

• Add fringe at the bottom that matches the color of the cross for a finished look.

Candidate for Ordination

[Jesus] said to His disciples, "The harvest is plentiful, but the laborers are few; therefore pray earnestly to the Lord of the harvest to send out laborers into His harvest." Matthew 9:37–38

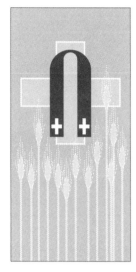 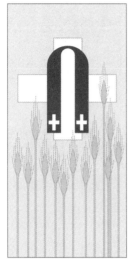

Tips & Extras · · · · · · · · · · · · · · · ·

- Red is the liturgical color for an ordination. Make the stole on this banner red.

- Make the background, cross, and wheat from earth-toned fabrics: tan, sage, off-white, brown, etc.

- If you can find it, consider using dried wheat or ornamental grass for the grain on this banner. Vary the heights of the grain to add visual interest.

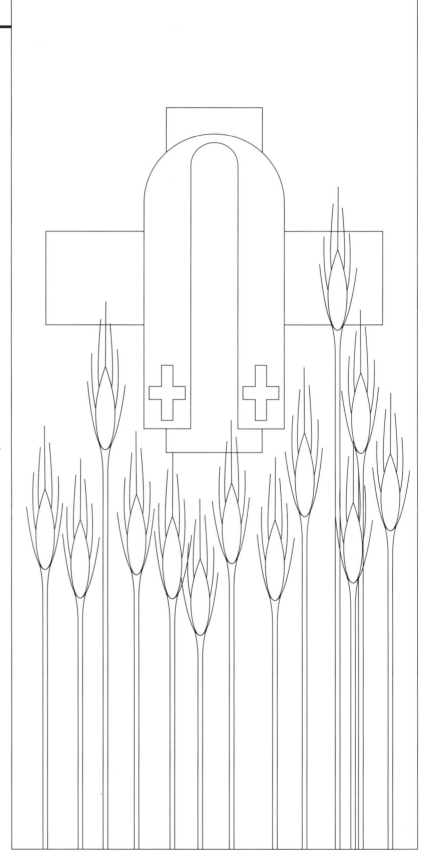

Installation/Ordination

Be steadfast, immovable, always abounding in the work of the Lord, knowing that in the Lord your labor is not in vain. 1 Corinthians 15:58

Tips & Extras ·····················

- Banner sample above left: With a wide brush, apply watered-down white glue in sweeping strokes, then sprinkle a combination of gold, silver, red glitter. Next, layer solid color yellow flames with a shadow of black.

- Banner sample above right: Give the flames visual texture by melting crayon shavings into yellow fabric. Use a warm iron on these items (in bottom to top order): ironing board, waxed paper, fabric, shavings, waxed paper. Try shavings in the white, yellow and orange color families. Cut out the shapes after melting the shavings. Use craft glue or hot glue to attach them.

- Include numerals to show what anniversary your pastor is celebrating. If you'd like to be able to reuse the banner for another anniversary, use a needle and thread to tack on the numbers and remove them later. To prevent the numbers from drooping, stiffen them first by lining with fusible interfacing.

10 15 20
30 40

Commissioning Anniversary

Teach me, O Lord, the way of Your statutes; and I will keep it to the end.
Psalm 119:33

Tips & Extras·······

- This banner is designed to celebrate "years of service" for Christian day school teachers. As shown, any number of anniversaries can be recognized at the same time, and the banners can be used again and again.

- The main banner will have a hanging casing at the top and the bottom, with rods in each that are 4" wider than the banner is wide. Each "years of service" banner also has casing at the top and the bottom. To hang banner to banner, use loops of cord around the rods themselves, through holes in the rods, or around screws in the ends of the rods. (See illustration below.)

- Use the school's colors predominantly.

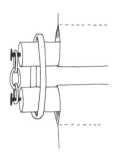

25

10

3456789

Elizabeth & Harold
June 17, 1962

12346

Therefore a man shall leave his father and his mother and hold fast to his wife, and they shall become one flesh.
Genesis 2:24

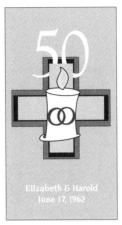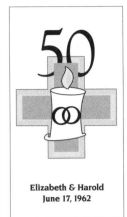

Tips & Extras ....

• This banner is appropriate for a vow renewal ceremony. Made smaller, it would also make a beautiful gift for a couple recognizing a significant wedding anniversary. This design could also be used for an embroidery pattern.

• For an elegant look, use all shades of white and gold, outlined with a dark color. The number should be the same dark color. The flame could be muted orange fabric.

• For a personal banner, add the couple's names and wedding date. For best results, follow the instructions for detailed letters on page 12.

Wedding Anniversary

Though a man might prevail against one who is alone, two will withstand him—a threefold cord is not quickly broken. Ecclesiastes 4:12

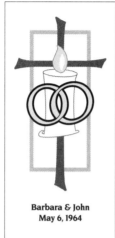

Tips & Extras

• Like the previous banner, this design is appropriate for a vow renewal ceremony. Made smaller, it would also make a beautiful gift for couple recognizing a significant wedding anniversary.

• Use a dark color for the cross, gold lamé for the rings, satin for the candle and flame.

• Use the layering technique to outline the rings. Start with a large darker colored shape, then add thinner rings on top.

• For a great gift, add the couple's names and wedding date. For best results, follow the instructions for detailed letters on page 12.

• This design could also be used for an embroidery pattern.

Barbara & John
May 6, 1964

PSALM 121;8

The LORD will keep your going out and your coming in from this time forth and forevermore. Psalm 121:8

psalm 121:8   psalm 121:8

Tips & Extras........

- The background could be two colors, or one color with "going out" and "coming in" formed in cord or ribbon.
- Use a subtle color for the cross. The staff, leaves, and dove should be the prominent elements.
- Include or omit the scripture reference as you wish.

Day School Teacher

The LORD bless you and keep you. The LORD make His face shine on you and be gracious to you. The LORD look upon you with favor and give you peace. Numbers 6:24–26

Tips & Extras

- When choosing fabrics, don't try to make everything stand out. Some elements have to be dominant or nothing will stand out.

- Make sure the lines in the hand that make the thumb and fingers are distinct enough to be seen from far away.

- The retirement banner designs could also be used as embroidery patterns. Add the retiree's name for a personalized gift.

Reception of New Members

"Truly I say to you, whoever does not receive the Kingdom of God like a child shall not enter it." And He took them in His arms and blessed them, laying His hands on them. Mark 10:15–16

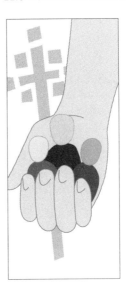 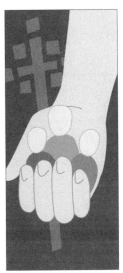

Tips & Extras ....

- Use different shades of fabric for the hand and faces.

- The three shirts should all be the same shade of fabric; all dark or all light, for example.

- Look at your in-progress banner from a distance. Depending on color choices, these elements might need to be heavily outlined.

- The seven squares surrounding the cross are for visual interest. Make them subtle by using a color very similar to the background.

Establishing a Congregation

So shall My word be that goes out from My mouth; it shall not return to Me empty, but it shall accomplish that which I purpose, and shall succeed in the thing for which I sent it.
Isaiah 55:11

Tips & Extras ················

- Use a dark fabric, or consider using dark shades of more than one color for the words. For best results in attaching the letters, follow the instructions on page 12.

- Use metallic fabrics for the shell, Bible, and chalice to contrast them against the words. Make the cross black. Use the layering technique to eliminate the need for outlining. Start with a large black shape and add colored shapes. (See below.)

- Trim the top and bottom edges of the banner with a strip of metallic fabric or ribbon to match the icon. Or use metallic cord and tassels for the hanging cord and matching fringe at the bottom.

My Word shall not return empty.

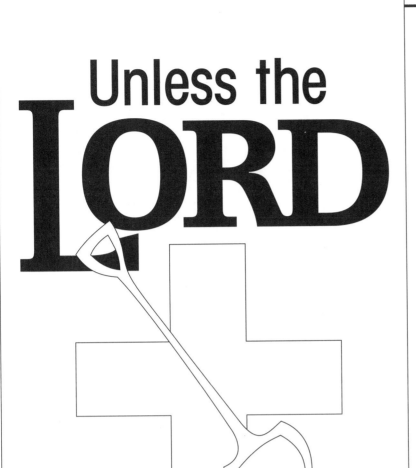

Unless the Lord builds the house, those who build it labor in vain. Psalm 127:1

Tips & Extras········

- This banner could be made for use during a groundbreaking ceremony. If a new sanctuary is being built, display the banner in the original sanctuary before the groundbreaking and in the new when it is completed.

- Choose a patterned fabric for the bottom portion of the banner, one that gives the appearance of soil or ground.

- Make the words "builds the house" the same color as the background.

- For best results in attaching the letters, follow the instructions on page 12.

Church Dedication

*I was glad when they said to me,
"Let us go to the house of the LORD!"
Psalm 122:1*

Tips & Extras

- Use a sponge and paint to stamp shapes like brick or stone on the fabric that makes the church.

- For best results with these letters, follow the instructions on page 12.

- Choose colors for the words that match your church's interior decorating.

- Balance the long shape of this banner with a long hanging rod and two long tassels on either side.

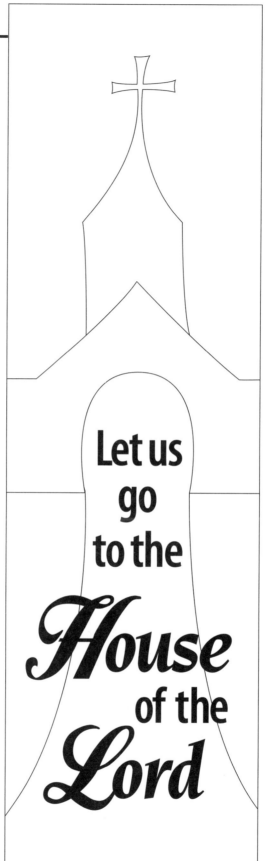

Let us
go
to the

House
of the
Lord

HOLY TRINITY LUTHERAN SCHOOL

AUGUST 8, 2018

Education Building or School Dedication

"You shall therefore lay up these words of Mine in your heart and in your soul . . . You shall teach them to your children, talking of them when you are sitting . . . , walking . . . , when you lie down, and when you rise." Deuteronomy 11:18–19

Tips & Extras

- Use this banner when dedicating a new education building or at the start of a new school year.

- Add your church's or school's name to the bottom of the banner, along with the date of the dedication or upcoming school term. Follow the instructions for detailed letters on page 12.

- For rays behind the cross: use three pieces of fabric to make three wide rays, or use cord or braid to make six thin rays.

- If the banner is for a school, use fabrics of the school's colors.

Hymns

Make a joyful noise to the LORD, all the earth; break forth into joyous song and sing praises! Psalm 98:4

Tips & Extras· · · · · · · · · · · · ·

• Make the harp from a metallic fabric.
• Several of these banners could be made and hung along the sides of the sanctuary. Make the "swoosh" behind the word "Joyful" a different color on each banner.
• Display this banner in the choir loft or music practice room.

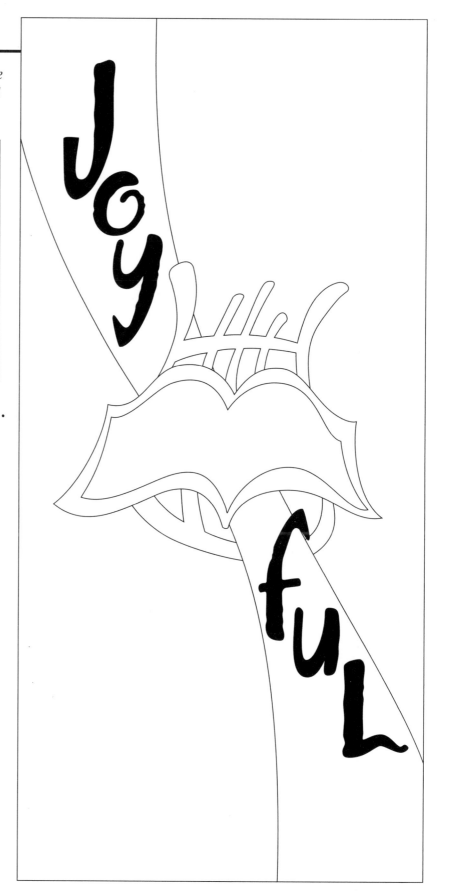

Athanasian Creed

Toward the end of the fifth century, this creed was written to delve into the mystery of the Trinity and clarify the beliefs of the true Christian Church.

Tips & Extras········· · · · · · ·

- Make the cross a metallic color or use a color similar to the background.
- The rings and triangle can be the same color or similar colors.
- The field at the top of the banner gives visual weight and balances the simplicity of the icon alone. Make it the same color as the triangle or rings.
- The easiest background fabric to use when making a rounded bottom banner is felt. It does not need to be hemmed or lined.

Kyrie Eleison

As (Jesus) was leaving Jerico with His disciples and a great crowd, Bartimaeus, a blind beggar, the son of Timaeus, was sitting by the roadside. And when he heard that it was Jesus of Nazareth, he began to cry out and say, "Jesus, Son of David, have mercy on me!"
Mark 10:46–47

Tips & Extras..................

- *Kyrie Eleison* is a greek phrase meaning "Lord, have mercy." This is an ancient expression used in many Christian liturgies.

- For a simplistic look, use one color paint or cord to outline the cross and sun shapes.

- For best results in working with these letters, follow the instructions on page 12.

- If you omit "Lord, have mercy," attach "Kyrie Eleison" in a slightly lower position. Before ironing, lay it out and look at it from a distance to make sure the banner doesn't look top-heavy.

- If the bottom of the banner ends in a point, finish with a tassel. Consider using a long hanging cord with matching tassels, as well.

Thanks be to God for His inexpressible gift! 2 Corinthians 9:15

Tips & Extras....................

- *Deo Gratia* is a Latin phrase meaning "Thanks be to God."

- If the cross and squares are made using a colored fabric, make the left/bottom edge of the banner the same color. Gold letters would look nice in this scheme.

- If the cross and squares are gold, use gold flat braid for the line that mimics the left/bottom edge of the banner. A dark or bright colored fabric would make letters that are easily legible. Use iron-on fusible for easy cutting and attaching.

- Trim and outline the cross until it's as fancy as you like.

Gloria Patri

Ascribe to the Lord the glory due His name; worship the Lord in the splendor of holiness. Psalm 29:2

Tips & Extras........

- *Gloria Patri* is a Latin phrase meaning "Glory be to the Father." It is an expression of praise used from the very early Christian church.

- The circle's outline behind the hand would look best as gold or silver lamé.

- When omitting "Glory be to the Father," lengthen the wrist to lower the illustration and words. This will visually balance and center everything on the banner.

- Add a tassel at the bottom point for a finishing touch.

The next day (John the Baptist) saw Jesus coming toward him, and said, "Behold, the Lamb of God, who takes away the sin of the world!" John 1:29

Tips & Extras · · · · · · · · · · · · · ·

- *Agnus Dei* (pronounced ahg-noose day) is a Latin phrase meaning "Lamb of God." The reference is to Jesus Christ, who was the perfect sacrificial offering for the salvation of all who believe in Him.

- Color option A: Make the cross gold lamé. Layer white fabric on black to make the lamb and its shadow. Outline the lamb with black squeeze paint as well. The words should be a bold color.

- Color option B: Make the cross a dark color and the background even darker. Layer white fabric on black to make the lamb and its shadow. The words could be white or gold lamé. Outline with squeeze paint to help the letters stand out more, if necessary.

- For best results in working with these letters, follow the instructions on page 12.

- If gold is used in the design, consider a gold border or fringe at the bottom to complement the gold fabric.

Pax

On the evening of that day, the first day of the week, the door being locked where the disciples were for fear of the Jews, Jesus came and stood among them and said to them, "Peace be with you." John 20:19

Tips & Extras

- *Pax* is the Latin word for "peace."

- The cross and squares will look striking if done in gold and bronze lamé. Trim the cross in black.

- The letters should be in sharp contrast to the background fabric. For best results in working with these letters, follow the instructions on page 12.

- The letters' drop shadow could be a lighter or darker shade of the letters themselves, or perhaps even a print in the letters' color family.

- Make the background of this banner very long to fit a long space in the chancel, an airy foyer, or near a stairway. Position the cross and letters about two-thirds of the way up from the banner's bottom.

Martin Luther's Seal

Tips & Extras·····························

- Martin Luther designed this seal as a visual representation of his faith. (c.1530) The following is a summary of the explanation of his design:

- The cross of black on a red heart serves as a reminder that faith in Jesus saves believers. The rose shows that faith gives joy, comfort and peace. It is white, for white is the color of angels. The sky blue field behind symbolizes the heavenly future joy. And around the field is a gold ring, which symbolizes the blessedness of heaven that has no end.

- One option, instead of using cord or paint to delineate the rose, is to layer the white rose on black fabric.

Martin Luther's Teaching

For by grace you have been saved through faith. And this is not your own doing; it is the gift of God, not a result of works, so that no one may boast. Ephesians 2:8–9

Tips & Extras

- Translated to English, these banners read, "Faith Alone, Grace Alone, Scripture Alone." This is one of Martin Luther's well-known teachings, presented here in Latin. Luther preached, and we believe today, what the scriptures teach, that salvation has been won for us through Jesus Christ. We receive eternal life only by God's grace that creates faith in what the Bible teaches—Jesus' redeeming work.

- The backgrounds for these three banners could all be the same color or similar colors in coordinating shades. The words and crosses should be the same color from one to another.

- For best results in working with these letters, follow the instructions on page 12.

- See "Tips & Extras" on page 87 to read about what colors to use for Luther's Seal.

- Trim the bottom of the banners with fringe to accentuate the group.

- Display these banners on a side wall of the sanctuary, hung perpendicular to the wall from brackets.

Sola Gratia

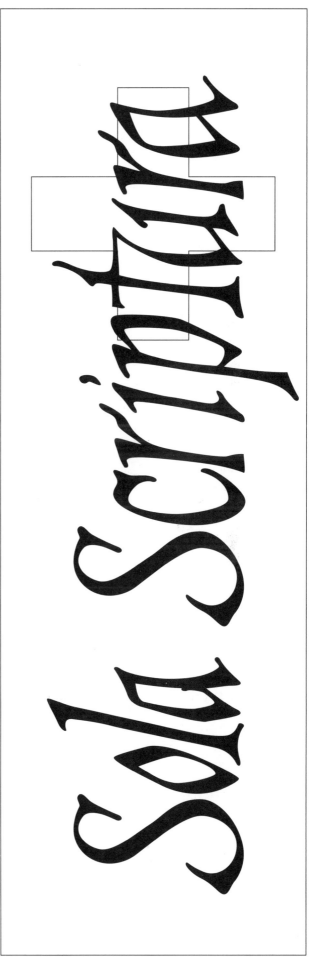

Sola Scriptura

AaBbCc

DdEeFf

GgHhIi

JjKkLl

-,;?Ww/

:MmNn
OPQRS
opqrsy
!Ttuvxz
UVXYZ

AaBbCc

DdEeFf

GgHhIi

JjKkLl

-;?Ww/

:MmNn
OPQRS
opqrsy
!Ttuvxz
UVXYZ

1 2 3 4 5

6 7 8 9 0

1 2 3 4 5

6 7 8 9 0

1 2 3 4 5

6 7 8 9 0